The Novel Notebook

One-page outlining and ideas workbook

The Novel Notebook
The Perfect Way to Record and Explore Ideas

ISBN: 978-1546896456

Created by Just Plan Books

As writers, we usually either have too many ideas or not enough. The Novel Notebook provides a solution to both of these problems. Storing ideas in these pages will allow you to work through them logically while also providing a record for later inspiration.

The front *Ideas* and *Notes* pages are intended to be a receptacle for all of your writing concepts, whatever form they take. An idea for a story, character, scene, or just a great sentence can go here for reference later.

When you have more time, use the One-Page Outline sheets to brainstorm and explore your idea in more detail.

The One-Page Outline sheets have been developed to be structured enough to guide you in the right direction, but simple enough to let your ideas roam and really take shape. If you're a *Pantser** this could be all the outline you need. If you're a *Plotter*** you'll probably want to develop the idea further.

* Pantser: A writer who writes without a detailed plan "flying by the seat of their pants".

** Plotter: A writer who plans everything to the very last detail.

Ideas

Ideas

Ideas

Notes

Ideas

Ideas

Ideas

Notes

Ideas

Ideas

Notes

Ideas

One-Page Outlines

One-Page Outline

Idea Summary

Characters

Beginning | Middle | End

Character Arc

Setting

Notes

One-Page Outline

Idea Summary

Characters

Beginning	Middle	End

Character Arc

Setting

Notes

One-Page Outline

Idea Summary

Characters

Beginning	Middle	End

Character Arc

Setting

Notes

One-Page Outline

Idea Summary

Characters

Beginning

Middle

End

Character Arc

Setting

Notes

One-Page Outline

Idea Summary

Characters

Beginning | Middle | End

Character Arc

Setting

Notes

One-Page Outline

Idea Summary

Characters

Beginning | Middle | End

Character Arc

Setting

Notes

One-Page Outline

Idea Summary

Characters

Beginning	Middle	End

Character Arc

Setting

Notes

One-Page Outline

Idea Summary

Characters

Beginning | Middle | End

Character Arc

Setting

Notes

One-Page Outline

Idea Summary

Characters

Beginning	Middle	End

Character Arc

Setting

Notes

One-Page Outline

Idea Summary

_____
_____
_____
_____

Characters

_____ _____ _____ _____
_____ _____ _____ _____
_____ _____ _____ _____
_____ _____ _____ _____
_____ _____ _____ _____

Beginning | Middle | End

_____ _____ _____
_____ _____ _____
_____ _____ _____
_____ _____ _____
_____ _____ _____
_____ _____ _____
_____ _____ _____
_____ _____ _____

Character Arc

_____ _____ _____
_____ _____ _____
_____ _____ _____
_____ _____ _____

Setting

_____ _____ _____
_____ _____ _____
_____ _____ _____
_____ _____ _____

Notes

_____
_____
_____
_____

One-Page Outline

Idea Summary

Characters

Beginning | Middle | End

Character Arc

Setting

Notes

One-Page Outline

Idea Summary

Characters

Beginning

Middle

End

Character Arc

Setting

Notes

One-Page Outline

Idea Summary

Characters

Beginning | Middle | End

Character Arc

Setting

Notes

One-Page Outline

Idea Summary

Characters

Beginning | Middle | End

Character Arc

Setting

Notes

One-Page Outline

Idea Summary

Characters

Beginning	Middle	End

Character Arc

Setting

Notes

One-Page Outline

Idea Summary

Characters

Beginning | Middle | End

Character Arc

Setting

Notes

One-Page Outline

Idea Summary

Characters

Beginning	Middle	End

Character Arc

Setting

Notes

One-Page Outline

Idea Summary

Characters

Beginning

Middle

End

Character Arc

Setting

Notes

One-Page Outline

Idea Summary

Characters

Beginning | Middle | End

Character Arc

Setting

Notes

One-Page Outline

Idea Summary

Characters

Beginning | Middle | End

Character Arc

Setting

Notes

One-Page Outline

Idea Summary

Characters

Beginning	Middle	End

Character Arc

Setting

Notes

One-Page Outline

Idea Summary

Characters

Beginning

Middle

End

Character Arc

Setting

Notes

One-Page Outline

Idea Summary

Characters

Beginning | Middle | End

Character Arc

Setting

Notes

One-Page Outline

Idea Summary

Characters

Beginning | Middle | End

Character Arc

Setting

Notes

One-Page Outline

Idea Summary

Characters

Beginning | Middle | End

Character Arc

Setting

Notes

One-Page Outline

Idea Summary

Characters

Beginning

Middle

End

Character Arc

Setting

Notes

One-Page Outline

Idea Summary

Characters

Beginning	Middle	End

Character Arc

Setting

Notes

One-Page Outline

Idea Summary

Characters

Beginning	Middle	End

Character Arc

Setting

Notes

One-Page Outline

Idea Summary

Characters

Beginning | Middle | End

Character Arc

Setting

Notes

One-Page Outline

Idea Summary

Characters

Beginning

Middle

End

Character Arc

Setting

Notes

One-Page Outline

Idea Summary

Characters

Beginning	Middle	End

Character Arc

Setting

Notes

One-Page Outline

Idea Summary

Characters

Beginning | Middle | End

Character Arc

Setting

Notes

One-Page Outline

Idea Summary

Characters

Beginning	Middle	End

Character Arc

Setting

Notes

One-Page Outline

Idea Summary

Characters

Beginning | Middle | End

Character Arc

Setting

Notes

One-Page Outline

Idea Summary

Characters

Beginning | Middle | End

Beginning	Middle	End

Character Arc

Setting

Notes

One-Page Outline

Idea Summary

Characters

Beginning

Middle

End

Character Arc

Setting

Notes

One-Page Outline

Idea Summary

Characters

Beginning | Middle | End

Character Arc

Setting

Notes

One-Page Outline

Idea Summary

Characters

Beginning | Middle | End

Character Arc

Setting

Notes

One-Page Outline

Idea Summary

Characters

Beginning | Middle | End

Character Arc

Setting

Notes

One-Page Outline

Idea Summary

Characters

Beginning | Middle | End

Character Arc

Setting

Notes

One-Page Outline

Idea Summary

Characters

Beginning | Middle | End

Character Arc

Setting

Notes

One-Page Outline

Idea Summary

Characters

Beginning | Middle | End

Character Arc

Setting

Notes

One-Page Outline

Idea Summary

Characters

Beginning | Middle | End

Character Arc

Setting

Notes

One-Page Outline

Idea Summary

Characters

Beginning | Middle | End

Character Arc

Setting

Notes

One-Page Outline

Idea Summary

Characters

Beginning | Middle | End

Character Arc

Setting

Notes

One-Page Outline

Idea Summary

Characters

Beginning	Middle	End

Character Arc

Setting

Notes

One-Page Outline

Idea Summary

Characters

Beginning | Middle | End

Beginning	Middle	End

Character Arc

Setting

Notes

One-Page Outline

Idea Summary

Characters

Beginning	Middle	End

Character Arc

Setting

Notes

One-Page Outline

Idea Summary

Characters

Beginning | Middle | End

Character Arc

Setting

Notes

One-Page Outline

Idea Summary

Characters

Beginning | Middle | End

Character Arc

Setting

Notes

One-Page Outline

Idea Summary

Characters

Beginning | Middle | End

Character Arc

Setting

Notes

One-Page Outline

Idea Summary

Characters

Beginning | Middle | End

Character Arc

Setting

Notes

One-Page Outline

Idea Summary

Characters

Beginning | Middle | End

Character Arc

Setting

Notes

One-Page Outline

Idea Summary

Characters

Beginning

Middle

End

Character Arc

Setting

Notes

One-Page Outline

Idea Summary

_____
_____
_____
_____

Characters

_____ | _____ | _____ | _____
_____ | _____ | _____ | _____
_____ | _____ | _____ | _____
_____ | _____ | _____ | _____
_____ | _____ | _____ | _____

Beginning	Middle	End

Character Arc

_____
_____
_____
_____

Setting

_____
_____
_____
_____

Notes

_____
_____
_____
_____

One-Page Outline

Idea Summary

Characters

Beginning | Middle | End

Character Arc

Setting

Notes

One-Page Outline

Idea Summary

Characters

Beginning | Middle | End

Character Arc

Setting

Notes

One-Page Outline

Idea Summary

Characters

Beginning | Middle | End

Character Arc

Setting

Notes

One-Page Outline

Idea Summary

Characters

Beginning | Middle | End

Character Arc

Setting

Notes

One-Page Outline

Idea Summary

Characters

Beginning | Middle | End

Character Arc

Setting

Notes

One-Page Outline

Idea Summary

Characters

Beginning | Middle | End

Character Arc

Setting

Notes

One-Page Outline

Idea Summary

Characters

Beginning | Middle | End

Character Arc

Setting

Notes

One-Page Outline

Idea Summary

Characters

Beginning | Middle | End

Character Arc

Setting

Notes

One-Page Outline

Idea Summary

Characters

Beginning	Middle	End

Character Arc

Setting

Notes

One-Page Outline

Idea Summary

Characters

Beginning | Middle | End

Character Arc

Setting

Notes

One-Page Outline

Idea Summary

Characters

Beginning	Middle	End

Character Arc

Setting

Notes

One-Page Outline

Idea Summary

Characters

Beginning	Middle	End

Character Arc

Setting

Notes

One-Page Outline

Idea Summary

Characters

Beginning	Middle	End

Character Arc

Setting

Notes

One-Page Outline

Idea Summary

Characters

Beginning	Middle	End

Character Arc

Setting

Notes

One-Page Outline

Idea Summary

Characters

Beginning

Middle

End

Character Arc

Setting

Notes

One-Page Outline

Idea Summary

Characters

Beginning | Middle | End

Character Arc

Setting

Notes

One-Page Outline

Idea Summary

Characters

Beginning / Middle / End

Beginning	Middle	End

Character Arc

Setting

Notes

One-Page Outline

Idea Summary

Characters

Beginning | Middle | End

Character Arc

Setting

Notes

One-Page Outline

Idea Summary

Characters

Beginning | Middle | End

Character Arc

Setting

Notes

One-Page Outline

Idea Summary

Characters

Beginning | Middle | End

Character Arc

Setting

Notes

One-Page Outline

Idea Summary

Characters

Beginning	Middle	End

Character Arc

Setting

Notes

One-Page Outline

Idea Summary

_____
_____
_____
_____

Characters

Beginning	Middle	End

Character Arc

_____
_____
_____
_____
_____

Setting

_____
_____
_____
_____
_____

Notes

_____
_____
_____
_____
_____

One-Page Outline

Idea Summary

Characters

Beginning | Middle | End

Character Arc

Setting

Notes

One-Page Outline

Idea Summary

Characters

Beginning | Middle | End

Character Arc

Setting

Notes

One-Page Outline

Idea Summary

Characters

Beginning	Middle	End

Character Arc

Setting

Notes

One-Page Outline

Idea Summary

Characters

Beginning | Middle | End

Character Arc

Setting

Notes

One-Page Outline

Idea Summary

Characters

Beginning

Middle

End

Character Arc

Setting

Notes

One-Page Outline

Idea Summary

Characters

Beginning	Middle	End

Character Arc

Setting

Notes

One-Page Outline

Idea Summary

Characters

Beginning	Middle	End

Character Arc

Setting

Notes

One-Page Outline

Idea Summary

Characters

Beginning | Middle | End

Character Arc

Setting

Notes

One-Page Outline

Idea Summary

Characters

Beginning | Middle | End

Character Arc

Setting

Notes

One-Page Outline

Idea Summary

Characters

Beginning | Middle | End

Character Arc

Setting

Notes

One-Page Outline

Idea Summary

Characters

Beginning | Middle | End

Character Arc

Setting

Notes

One-Page Outline

Idea Summary

Characters

Beginning	Middle	End

Character Arc

Setting

Notes

One-Page Outline

Idea Summary

Characters

Beginning

Middle

End

Character Arc

Setting

Notes

One-Page Outline

Idea Summary

Characters

Beginning | Middle | End

Character Arc

Setting

Notes

Idea Summary

Characters

Beginning | Middle | End

Character Arc

Setting

Notes

One-Page Outline

Idea Summary

Characters

Beginning | Middle | End

Character Arc

Setting

Notes

One-Page Outline

Idea Summary

Characters

Beginning | ## Middle | ## End

Character Arc

Setting

Notes

One-Page Outline

Idea Summary

Characters

Beginning | Middle | End

Character Arc

Setting

Notes

One-Page Outline

Idea Summary

Characters

Beginning | Middle | End

Character Arc

Setting

Notes

One-Page Outline

Idea Summary

Characters

Beginning | Middle | End

Character Arc

Setting

Notes

One-Page Outline

Idea Summary

Characters

Beginning	Middle	End

Character Arc

Setting

Notes

One-Page Outline

Idea Summary

Characters

Beginning	Middle	End

Character Arc

Setting

Notes

One-Page Outline

Idea Summary

Characters

Beginning | Middle | End

Character Arc

Setting

Notes

61774806R00073

Made in the USA
San Bernardino, CA
16 December 2017